THE BENGAL ROSE PRINCESS

BY

Lloyd E Bateman

Dedication

This book would not have been written without encouragement from my wonderful "Neighbors from across the River" Sarah Stewart Small and David Small. Both of them are very accomplished children's books authors in their own rights

Some words we need to know:

Privy: A toilet located in a small shed outside a house or other building; an outhouse Feline: A cat or other member of the cat family. Much superstitions surrounds cats. Some say cats have 9 lives.

The story behind the Story

My dreams...ever fanciful. However none of my dreams compare to the one that brought me the story of the "Bengal Rose Princess".

That night, in that dream and in the following day, things happened that are to me, to this day still unexplainable. Upon awakening, I realized immediately that I had witnessed something extraordinary and began researching and making notes of the revelations that flowed to me from it.

I felt for a fact that the young man whose name was Yang Lee, another orphan taken in by the Emperor, was me and I knew it in my core. I knew I was living in the Tang Dynasty and that the "child" Rose who I have since regarded as the spirit of a young tigress was very real to me.

I knew the roses in that garden were called Bengal Roses. That was subsequently verified by me that same day. I have no recollection of ever hearing about the China Rose or Bengal Rose before.

After a quick breakfast and coffee, I began writing the story. Perhaps I should say transcribing the story, since it already seemed written as it came to me. Trite? Yes, but although I have some experience writing, I never wrote poetry and it poured out effortlessly for the next twelve or so hours. The story was complete; every detail from the dream was there. Of course I did massage the words and completed many rewrites over time, but the essence was there complete from the start.

I hope you enjoy reading "The Bengal Rose Princess" as much as I have enjoyed bringing her to you.

Yours very sincerely, Lloyd E Bateman

A child princess named the Bengal Rose appeared in the garden without any clothes.

They looked for her parents both high and low, but all who they asked, just said (No).

繡暉閣

Everyone marveled at her eyes and her hair as the mark of the tiger surely lie there.

The royal family soon made a decree, that this young child now a Princess would be.

I am Yang Lee a child of this place;Bengal Rose with a kiss placed her hands on my face.

You are me and I am of you, you'll be my champion, that's what you'll do.

So I tell you the story both happy and sad, just wait til the end...you'll surely be glad.

Everyone loved the Bengal Rose from the top of her head to the tips of her toes.

She displayed very quickly her gifts of the cat and all were amazed at how she did that.

At an age of just four through her balance and grace, all who had gathered had a smile on their face.

The Emperor's child of the Garden, the Bengal Rose, became the sensation now everyone knows.

On the high wire she danced, did some flips and some flops. All could see now that she was the tops.

From the grown-up wire walker no jealousy came, as she always knew it was a part of the game.

But there was another, all filled with hate, who wanted Rose dead for sealing her fate.

He loved the grown wire walker but she never knew as he'd never shown her or knew what to do.

Rose and I were "living the dream" when one day she yelled "let's go get ice cream!"

So to town we did go for that special treat dancing and singing all the way down the street.

When we got home, the Emperor was mad he said "I was so worried and I was so sad."

"Don't you know of the danger just lurking outside? We must never

forget that she could have died!"

We must hide her and move her now every day for the rumors insist she'll be taken away.

So we ran and we moved every day, except to perform or if alright to play.

Now, so sorry I tell you of the day that she died. For it was the day that our whole world cried.

Rose said to me "I've got to go pee."

So we both ran fast to the nearest privy.

I left her alone for her private space when the door flew open very hard in my face.

I fell so hard that all I could see was a shapeless black form taking Rose from me.

He dove in the river with her in his arm there was no way to stop him from doing her harm.

The formless black being had forced her to drown, and although we did search, she never was found.

The love for the Princess was shown everywhere with chanting and singing and in silent prayer.

A full year had passed now with flowers full bloom, like Rose's first day, twas the end of the gloom.

加拉玫瑰
ngal Rose
Bengal Rose

The Bengal Rose Princess was like a feline. And the lives

that she had in total were nine.

The river she drowned in flowed back to the flowers, and now in life number two

she was ours.

Skipping and dancing came the child.

Bengal Rose and so as before without any clothes.

More than friends:

Thank you again for all your support and suggestions to help me get "unstuck" when working out all the details of the illustrations and in bringing to fruition my dream.

Rachelle A Secson

Kirsten Neeley Lawes

Birtha Melody Belmont